|| ॐ गुरुपराय न

om guruparāya nama

Shanti Mantras

Reflective thoughts to pacify human suffering

Patanjali Kundalini Yoga~Care

With devanagari, transliteration, word-by-word English translation, and verse meaning.

Published by:
PKYC
Patanjali Kundalini Yoga~Care
Offering individualized spiritual guidance for seekers on any path

KundaliniCare.com
Kundalini@KundaliniCare.com
PKYC: Rishikesh, India & Knoxville, TN

ISBN 0-9710128-3-0
Printed 2015

Shanti Mantras

The treasures of knowledge of Sanatana Dharma, the ancient teachings of the Vedic *rishis*, are the four Vedas. The last portion of each Veda is called *Upanisad*, scriptures that are the source of Vedanta philosophy. Every Upanisad begins with an invocation ending with the word *shanti*, which means peace. These are the shanti mantras. *Mantra* means to cultivate and improve reflective thoughts. The shanti mantras are reflections on that which brings peace. The recitation of the shanti mantras of the Vedas in Sanskrit enhances concentration of the mind and creates a meditative atmosphere within and without. This is made by the tranquil vibration radiating from the Self-Illumination that shines on our Intellect, *Buddhi*. In Sanskrit, the sounds of the words are arranged to go with the rhythm of singing, thereby strengthening the power of the phoneme vibrations. Chanting these mantras brings the revelation of Absolute Reality through discrimination and dispassion as well as spiritual discipline, morality, and nobility.

Every human being looks for ways to pacify the chaos of human life. But if they are looking outside, they will be disappointed. The reflective thought promoted by concentrating on the shanti mantras helps us to be free of the dense rolling darkness of our inner chaos. The shanti mantras help us to be more aware of the Inner Light that can soothe and ease our human plight.

These mantras encourage the mind to ask Absolute Reality to reveal the light of Self-awareness. The spiritual practice of chanting the shanti mantras aloud combines the use of positive speech, regulated breath, concentrated mind, and spiritual yearning. The powerful yet gentle vibration of the vocalized Sanskrit phonemes is beneficial to brain function, promoting physical relaxation, improved neurotransmitter production, and emotional upliftment.

Impulsive and instinctive thought patterns form neural pathways that predispose us to certain emotional reactions. The way we think forms the way we feel, and that affects the way we act. The prefrontal cortex, which is the seat of reason, is directly connected to the limbic system, the seat of raw emotion, and can inhibit the animal reactivity of the amygdala. Our higher awareness, our outlook, can change our temperament and moods. Systematic mental practices reroute negative pathways, freeing us to be more resilient, focused, aware, and peaceful. Chanting the shanti mantras is a powerful and sacred way to calm the agitated inner beast. With practice, the mental training inherent in chanting can change the neural structure and function of the brain in fundamentally beneficial ways, providing increased emotional balance and peace.

It is recommended that you begin and end the day by chanting these peace mantras, and you can also chant them anytime the mind feels disturbed. Chant with reverent awareness, inhaling fully and allowing the sounds to flow out in a robust yet gentle manner. Feel the vibration of the sounds as they resonate in your body and mind. Chant them as heartfelt aspirations.

This booklet is designed to help you learn to read and pronounce these holy mantras, chanting along with the matching *Shanti Mantras* CD. It is laid out so you can easily view the Sanskrit in devanagari script with its transliteration placed just below it and the word by word translation aligned under that. This allows you to learn the pronunciation of the words while understanding their meanings. The line meaning is provided under these, and the meaning of the whole verse is presented on the facing page of each mantra.

To assist in easy identification, the shanti mantras presented here have been given numbers and names in English:

1. Yo vai brahmāṇam:	Call for Guidance to the Source
2. Vāṅ me manasi:	Request for Wisdom and Protection
3. Bhadram karṇebhiḥ:	Petition for Auspiciousness
4. Sahanāvavatu:	Student Teacher Agreement
5. Yaś chandasām:	Request for Knowledge of Reality
6. Bhadram no api:	Asking for Peaceful Adjuncts
7. Aham vṛkṣasya:	Trishanku's Declaration
8. Śam no mitraḥ:	Praise and Prostrations
9. Āpyāyantu:	Plea for Strength and Virtue
10. Pūrṇamadaḥ:	Proclamation of Perfection

NOTE:

In Sanskrit, some combinations of words render a change in sound at the juncture of the words. This is called *sandhi,* meaning "coalescence." Sandhi rules help to regulate the flow of prana during recitation. To facilitate pronunciation and understanding by aspirants who are unfamiliar with Sanskrit, we have divided the devanagari script and the transliterated words for pedagogic purposes. We ask Sanskrit scholars to forgive the utilitarian freedoms we have taken with word divisions and sandhi rules. The original unbroken devanagari can be found at the end of the booklet, as can the translated and transliterated verses. Transliterated components of compounds are presented "pre-sandhi" here so the student can understand the meaning of the words. Compounds are indicated in the transliteration with a hyphen between the combined words. The sandhi combinations are left intact in the devanagari.

As some Sanskrit words are very difficult to translate into English, we have retained Anglicized versions of them in our translation. The following brief glossary defines these special terms listed without the standard diacritical marks:

Amrita — The immortal nectar of spiritual knowledge.

Ananda — The positive experience beyond body and mind.

Atman — The individual Self, the Absolute Reality within.

Brahman — The universal Self, the all-pervading Absolute Reality.

Buddhi — The discriminative faculty, the higher Intellect.

Deva — A holy bright being of light, beyond the physical realm.

Karmasaya — Collected deeply imprinted experiences and desires from the past.

Prana — The vital life force animating body, senses, mind, and Intellect (Buddhi).

Rishi — An ancient seer who conveys the revealed spiritual Truth in scripture.

Samskara — A past impression carried in the mind; a thought groove.

Sattva — The peaceful, light, wise aspect of nature.

Shanti — Peace.

The Transliteration of Sanskrit

This chart is offered as a general orientation to the Sanskrit alphabet. Sanskrit is a phonetic language, and correct pronunciation of the phonemes is considered to be essential to the effect they have on the practitioner's subtle system. Some Sanskrit sounds have no English equivalent, so the nearest approximate sound in English has been offered.

Vowels:

अ a but	आ ā father	इ i it	ई ī petite	उ u put	ऊ ū rude	ऋ ṛ rhythm	ॠ ṝ marine
ए e fiancé	ऐ ai aisle	ओ o go	औ au frau	अं ṁ hum	अः ḥ aha	ऌ ḷ lyric	ॡ ḹ revelry
				(Anusvara)	(Visarga)		

Consonants:

Gutterals:	क ka karate	ख kha work hut	ग ga gut	घ gha log hut	ङ ṅa sing
Palatals:	च ca cello	छ cha catch him	ज ja jutt	झ jha hedge hog	ञ ña onion
Cerebrals:	ट ṭa water	ठ ṭha lighthouse	ड ḍa drum	ढ ḍha mud hut	ण ṇa under
Dentals:	त ta tub	थ tha boat hut	द da duck	ध dha adhere	न na nut
Labials:	प pa putt	फ pha uphill	ब ba but	भ bha abhor	म ma mum
Semi-vowels:	य ya yes	र ra run	ल la luck	व va vodka	
Silibants:	श śa shawl	ष ṣa shun	स sa saw	ह ha hunch	
Conjunctions:	क्ष kṣa black ship	त्र tra trip	ज्ञ jña Guyana		

The Sanskrit alphabet letters are presented here in their traditional order. Sanskrit vowels are short or long (indicated by a line over the vowel). Consonants are simple or aspirated (indicated by an "h" after the consonant). These are pronounced with a puff of exhaled air. Consonants are arranged according to their locus of articulation from the back of the throat to the front of the mouth. Cerebrals (retroflexives, shown with dots under) are pronounced by placing the tip of the tongue on the ridge of the hard palate. Dentals are pronounced by placing the tongue on the back of the upper teeth, a bit lower than in English.

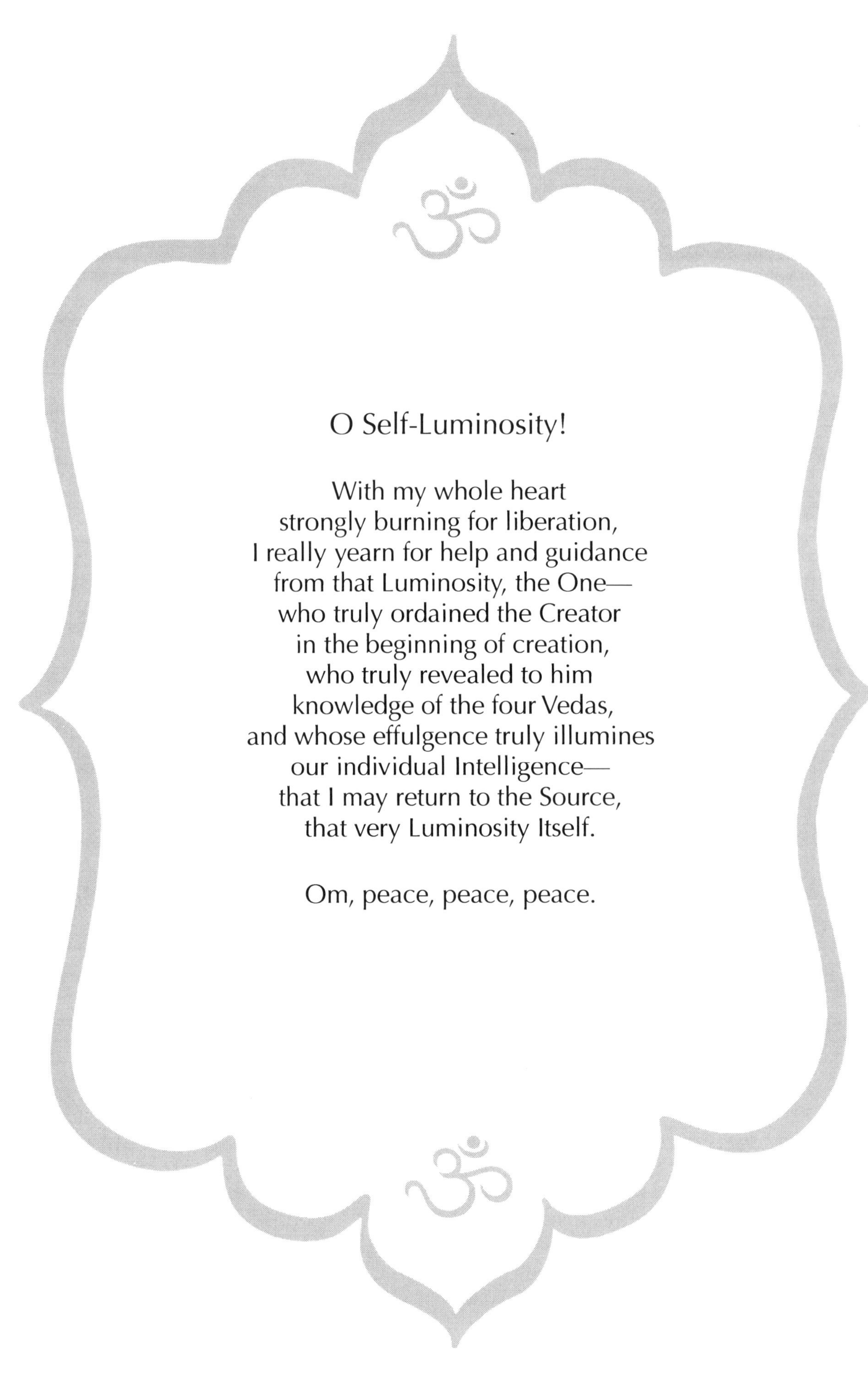

O Self-Luminosity!

With my whole heart
strongly burning for liberation,
I really yearn for help and guidance
from that Luminosity, the One—
who truly ordained the Creator
in the beginning of creation,
who truly revealed to him
knowledge of the four Vedas,
and whose effulgence truly illumines
our individual Intelligence—
that I may return to the Source,
that very Luminosity Itself.

Om, peace, peace, peace.

1. Call for Guidance to the Source

ॐ
om
O Self-Luminosity!

यो वै ब्रह्माणम् विदधाति पूर्वम्
yo vai brahmāṇam vidadhāti pūrvam
who- really- the Creator- ordains- in the past (in the beginning of creation)
who truly ordained the Creator in the beginning of creation,

यो वै वेदांश् च प्रहिणोति तस्मै ।
yo vai vedāṁś- ca prahiṇoti tasmai,
who- really- knowledge of the Veda- and- reveals- to him
who truly revealed to him knowledge of the four Vedas,

तम् ह देवम् आत्म बुद्धि प्रकाशम् ॥
tam ha devam- ātma- buddhi- prakāśam.
to whom- with my heart- effulgence- the individual Self- the Intelligence of- is enlightening and whose effulgence truly illumines our individual Intelligence–

मुमुक्षुर् वै शरणम् अहम् प्रपद्ये ॥
mumukṣur- vai śaraṇam- aham prapadye.
strong burning for liberation- with sincerity- for help and guidance- I am- seeking
With my whole heart strongly burning for liberation, I really yearn for help and guidance (from that Luminosity, the One–that I may return to the Source, that very Luminosity Itself).

ॐ शान्तिः शान्तिः शान्तिः
om śāntiḥ śāntiḥ śāntiḥ
Om, peace, peace, peace.

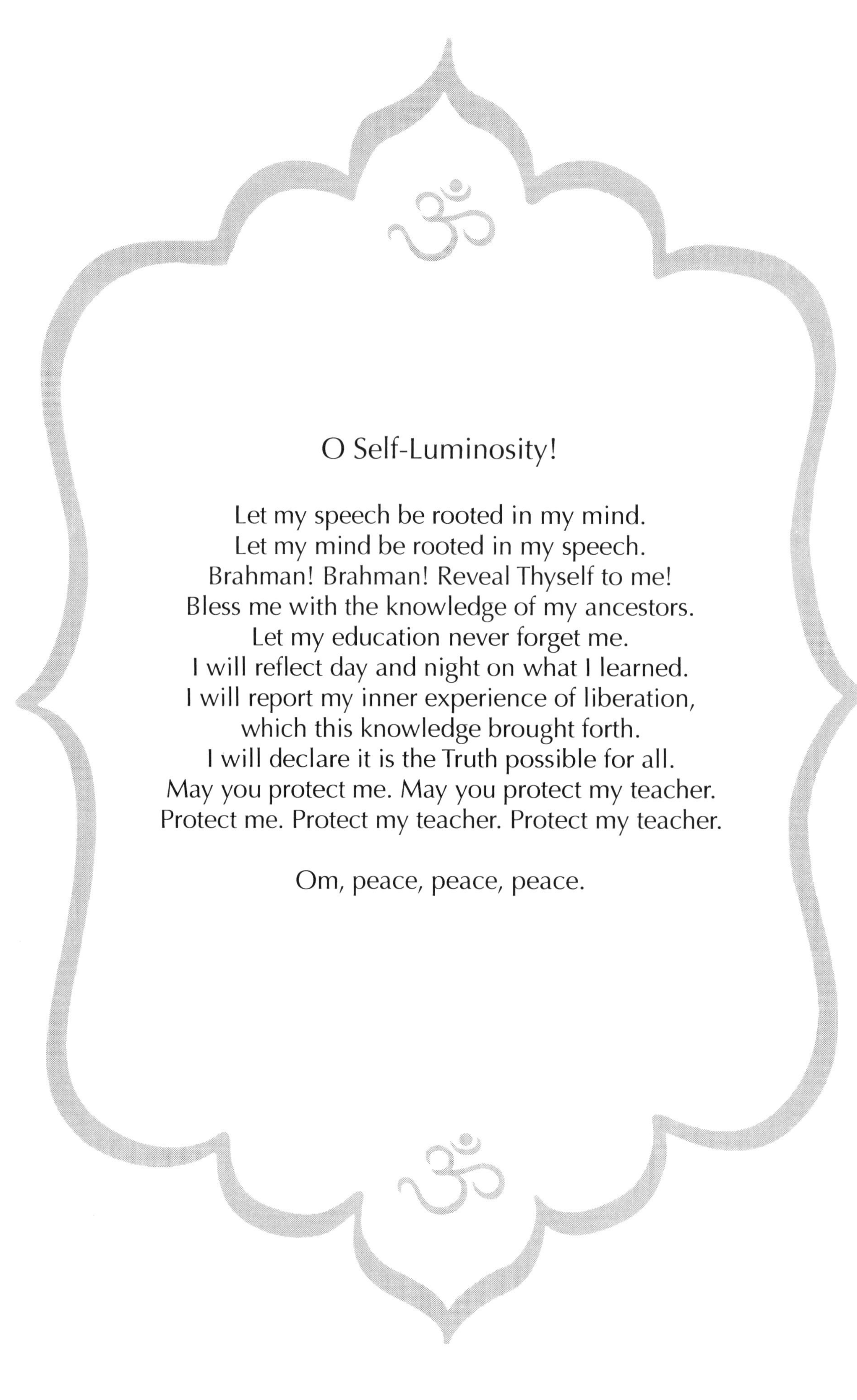

O Self-Luminosity!

Let my speech be rooted in my mind.
Let my mind be rooted in my speech.
Brahman! Brahman! Reveal Thyself to me!
Bless me with the knowledge of my ancestors.
Let my education never forget me.
I will reflect day and night on what I learned.
I will report my inner experience of liberation,
which this knowledge brought forth.
I will declare it is the Truth possible for all.
May you protect me. May you protect my teacher.
Protect me. Protect my teacher. Protect my teacher.

Om, peace, peace, peace.

2. Request for Wisdom and Protection

ॐ
om
O Self-Luminosity!

वाङ् मे मनसि प्रतिष्ठिता मनो मे वाचि प्रतिष्ठितम्
vāṅ- me manasi pratiṣṭhitā mano me vāci pratiṣṭhitam-
speech- my- with mind- associate mind- my- with speech- associate
Let my speech be rooted in my mind. Let my mind be rooted in my speech.

आविर् आविर् म एधि। वेदस्य मा आणीस्थः
āvir- āvir- ma edhi, vedasya mā āṇīsthaḥ
Brahman- Brahman- to me- reveal yourself knowledge of ancestors- me- educate
Brahman! Brahman! Reveal Thyself to me! Bless me with the knowledge of my ancestors.

श्रुतम् मे मा प्रहासीर् अनेन अधीतेन अहोरात्रान् सन्दधामि
śrutam me mā prahāsīr- anena-adhītena- ahorātrān- sandadhāmi
knowledge I heard- me- not- forget that I learned- day and night- reflect
Let my education never forget me. I will reflect day and night on what I learned.

ऋतम् वदिष्यामि। सत्यं वदिष्यामि
ṛtam vadiṣyāmi, satyam vadiṣyāmi
inner experience- I will tell truth- I will tell That (Absolute Reality)
I will report my inner experience, which this knowledge brought forth.
I will declare it is the Truth possible for all.

तन् माम् अवतु तद् वक्तारम् अवतु। अवतु माम् अवतु वक्तारम् अवतु वक्तारम्॥
tan-mām- avatu tad- vaktāram- avatu, avatu mām- avatu vaktāram avatu vaktāram.
me- protect that- teacher- protect, protect- me protect- teacher protect- teacher
May you protect me. May you protect my teacher. Protect me.
Protect my teacher. Protect my teacher.

ॐ शान्तिः शान्तिः शान्तिः
om śāntiḥ śāntiḥ śāntiḥ
Om, peace, peace, peace.

O Self-Luminosity!

O adorable devas, beings of light!
May my ears always hear what is auspicious.
May my eyes always see what is auspicious.
I glorify you with my strong body and mind.
May I live in the way of Illumination
for all of my allotted lifetime.

Om, peace, peace, peace.

3. Petition for Auspiciousness

ॐ

om

O Self-Luminosity!

भद्रम्	कर्णेभिः	शृणुयाम	देवाः ।
bhadram	karṇebhiḥ	śṛṇuyāma	devāḥ,
auspicious-	by ears-	let me hear-	light beings

May my ears always hear what is auspicious, O beings of light!

भद्रम्	पश्येम	अक्षभिर्	यजत्राः ।
bhadram	paśyema-	akṣabhir-	yajatrāḥ,
auspicious-	by eyes-	let me see-	adorable ones

May my eyes always see what is auspicious, O adorable ones.

स्थिरैर्	अंगैस्	तुष्टुवांगम्	सस्तनुभिः ।
sthirair-	aṅgais-	tuṣṭuvāṅ-gam-	sastanūbhiḥ,
with	strong limbs-	I glorify-	with body

I glorify you with my strong body and mind.

व्यशेम	देवहितम्	यदायुः ॥
vyaśema	deva-hitam	yad-āyuḥ.
I live-	in way of Illumination-	allotted- lifetime

May I live in the way of Illumination for all of my allotted lifetime.

ॐ शान्तिः शान्तिः शान्तिः

om śāntiḥ śāntiḥ śāntiḥ

Om, peace, peace, peace.

O Self-Luminosity!

May we both be protected.
May we both grow and improve together.
May we both have strong motivation for our endeavor.
May our knowledge brightly shine, and
May we thus always have harmony
in our life together.

Om, peace, peace, peace.

4. Student Teacher Agreement

ॐ
om
O Self-Luminosity!

सह नाववतु । सह नौ भुनक्तु ।
saha nāvavatu, saha nau bhunaktu,
both- us protect both- us- grow/improve
May we both be protected. May we both grow and improve together.

सह वीर्यम् करवावहै । तेजस्वि न अवधी तम् अस्तु
saha vīryam karavāvahai, tejasvi na- avadhī- tam- astu
both- strong- motivation be bright- us- our study,
May we both have strong motivation for our endeavor.
May our knowledge brightly shine.

मा विद्विषावहै ॥
mā vidviṣāvahai.
not- disturb the harmony
May we thus always have harmony in our life together.

ॐ शान्तिः शान्तिः शान्तिः
om śāntiḥ śāntiḥ śāntiḥ
Om, peace, peace, peace.

O Self-Luminosity!

As the bull is in the cow herd,
so the monosyllable om is in the Vedic hymns.
You are all-pervasive, the manifest knowledge of Immortality.
Like Indra, may I be prosperous with the knowledge of Reality.
O deva, bright being of Light!
Let me be the repository of the knowledge of immortality.
Let my body be strong for the spiritual endeavor.
Let my tongue be full of delight.
Let me be ananda, the experience beyond mind and senses.
Let my ears hear abundantly.
O Luminosity, you are clothed with sattvic wisdom.
These manifest adjuncts veil you,
but the knowledge of Reality adorns you.
Let me preserve what I have learned and
apply it to attain the goal.

Om, peace, peace, peace.

5. Request for Knowledge of Reality

ॐ

om

O Self-Luminosity!

यश्	छन्दसाम्	ऋषभो	विश्वरूपः ॥
yaś	chandasām-	ṛṣabho	viśvarūpaḥ.
which-	among the hymns	most excellent bull-	all pervasive-

You are all-pervasive, most excellent among the Vedic hymns,

छन्दोभ्यो	अध्यमृतात्	संबभूव ।	समेन्द्रो	मेधया	स्पृणोतु ॥
chandobhyo-	adhyamṛtāt	sambabhūva,	samendro	medhayā	spṛṇotu.
from the hymns-	immortal nectar-	manifested.	Like Indra-	knowledge of Reality-	make prosperous

manifested from the great nectar of immortality. Like Indra, may I be prosperous.

अमृतस्य	देव	धारणो	भूयासम् ॥
amṛtasya	deva	dhāraṇo	bhūyāsam.
of nectar	bright ones-	repository-	let me be

(the knowledge of immortality)

O Illumination! Let me be the repository of spiritual knowledge.

शरीरम्	मे	विचर्षणम् ॥	जिह्वा	मे	मधु मत्तमा ॥
śarīram	me	vicarṣaṇam.	jihvā	me	madhu mattamā.
body-	my-	let be strong	tongue-	my-	delight- full of

Let my body be strong for the spiritual endeavor. Let my tongue be full of delight.
(Let me be ananda, the experience beyond mind and senses.)

कर्णाभ्याम्	भूरि	विश्रुवम् ॥	ब्रह्मणः	कोशोऽसि	मेधया	पिहितः ॥
karṇābhyām	bhūri	viśruvam.	brahmaṇaḥ	kośo'si	medhayā	pihitaḥ.
let my ears-	abundantly-	hear	of Brahman-	veil-	you are pure	clothed with-

Let my ears hear abundantly. You are clothed with sattvic wisdom.
These manifest adjuncts veil you, but the knowledge of Reality adorns you.

श्रुतम्	मे	गोपाय ॥
śrutam	me	gopāya.
verses/education-	me-	preserve

Let me preserve what I have learned and apply it to attain the goal.

ॐ शान्तिः शान्तिः शान्तिः

om śāntiḥ śāntiḥ śāntiḥ

Om, peace, peace, peace.

O Self-Luminosity!

May our body,
senses, prana, mind,
and Intellect
be good to us.

Om, peace, peace, peace.

6. Asking for Peaceful Adjuncts

ॐ

om

O Self-Luminosity!

भद्रम नो अपिवातय मनः ||

bhadram no apivātaya manaḥ

good- to us- let it be- mind

May our body, senses, prana, mind, and Intellect be good to us.

ॐ शान्तिः शान्तिः शान्तिः

om śāntiḥ śāntiḥ śāntiḥ

Om, peace, peace, peace.

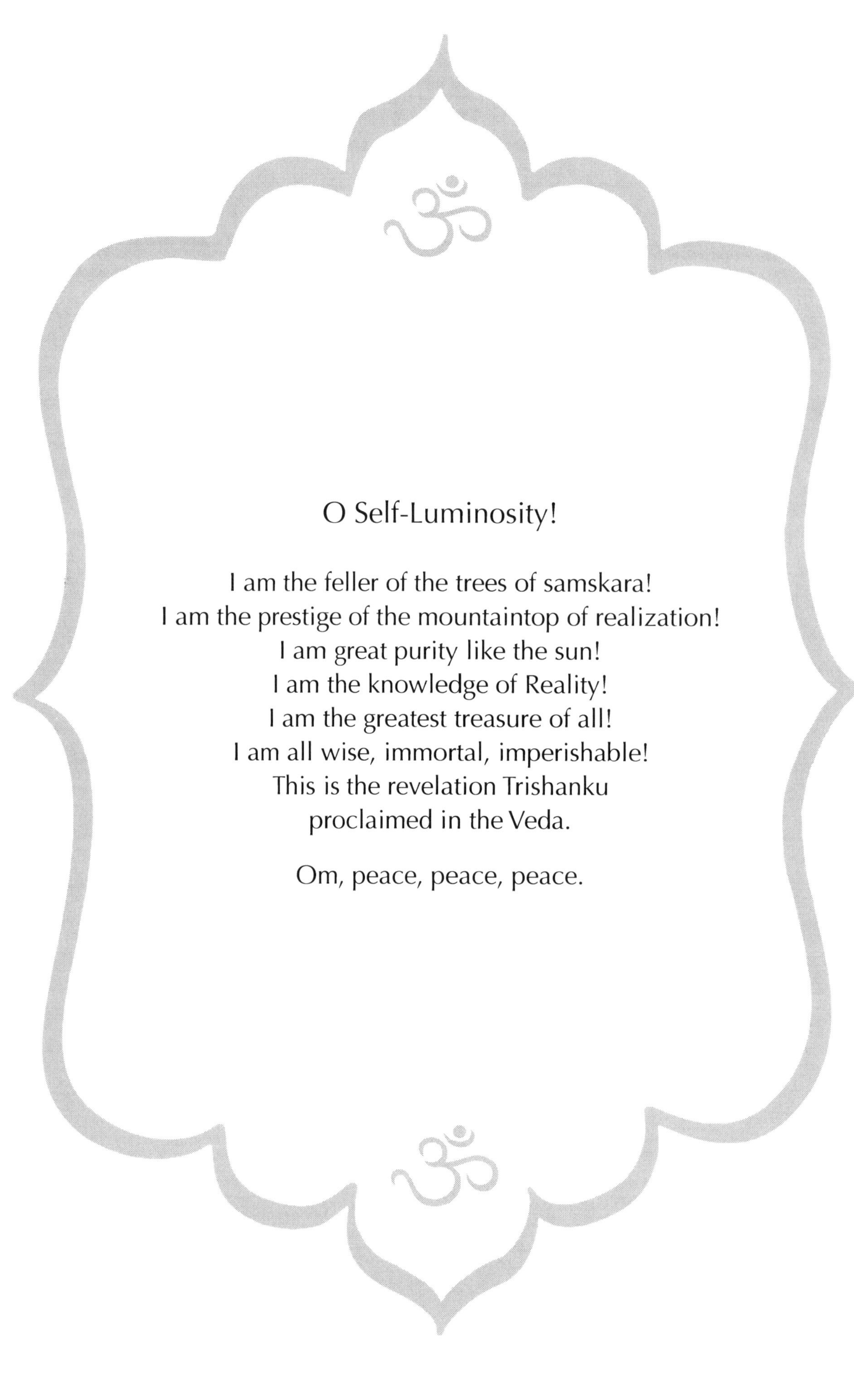

O Self-Luminosity!

I am the feller of the trees of samskara!
I am the prestige of the mountaintop of realization!
I am great purity like the sun!
I am the knowledge of Reality!
I am the greatest treasure of all!
I am all wise, immortal, imperishable!
This is the revelation Trishanku
proclaimed in the Veda.

Om, peace, peace, peace.

7. Trishanku's Declaration

ॐ
om
O Self-Luminosity!

अहम् वृक्षस्य रेरिव। कीर्त्तिः पृष्ठम् गिरेर् इव।
aham vṛkśasya reriva, kīṛttiḥ pṛṣṭham girer- iva,
I am- of tree- destroyer- prestige- peak- of the mountain
I am the feller of the trees of samskara! I am the prestige of the mountaintop of realization!

ऊर्ध्व पवित्रो वाजिनीव स्वम् ऋतम् अस्मि।
ūrdhva pavitro vājini-iva svam- ṛtam- asmi,
great- purity- sun-like- self- knowledge of Reality- I am
I am great purity like the sun! I am the knowledge of Reality!

द्रविणम् सवर्चसम्। सुमेधा अमृतो ऽ क्षितः।
draviṇam savarcasam, sumedhā amṛto ' kṣitaḥ,
treasure- of all- highest all wise- immortal-imperishable-
I am the greatest treasure of all! I am all wise, immortal, imperishable!

इति त्रिशंकोर् वेद अनुवाचनम्॥
iti triśaṅkor- veda- anūvācanam.
this- Trishanku's- Veda- testimonial
This is the revelation Trishanku proclaimed in the Veda.

ॐ शान्तिः शान्तिः शान्तिः
om śāntiḥ śāntiḥ śāntiḥ
Om, peace, peace, peace.

O Self-Luminosity!

Morning sun, be good to us.
Midday sun, be good to us.
Evening sun, be good to us.
Indra, king of the devas, be good to us.
Brihaspati, Lord of knowledge, be good to us.
Vishnu, the all-pervasive, grant us speedy progress.
Prostrations to Absolute Reality!
Prostrations to Vayu, the prana,
who is really the visible Absolute Reality.
Really, I proclaim prana is the visible Brahman.
I declare my inner experience is Truth.
I declare it is Truth always for all.
May you protect me. May you protect the teacher.
Protect me. Protect the teacher.

Om, peace, peace, peace.

8. Praise and Prostrations

ॐ
om
O Self-Luminosity!

शम् नो मित्रः शम् वरुणः । शम् नो भवत् वर्यमा ।
śaṁ no mitraḥ śaṁ varuṇaḥ, śaṁ no bhavat- varyamā,
good- to us- morning sun, good- midday sun good- to us- let it be -setting sun
Morning sun, be good to us. Midday sun, be good to us. Evening sun, be good to us.

शम् न इन्द्रो बृहस्पतिः । शम् नो विष्णुर् उरुक्रमः ।
śaṁ na indro bṛhaspatiḥ, śaṁ no viṣṇur- urukramaḥ,
good- to us- Indra Brihaspati good- to us- Vishnu of great strides
Indra, king of the devas, be good to us. Brihaspati, Lord of knowledge, be good to us.
Vishnu, the all-pervasive, grant me speedy progress.

नमो ब्रह्मणे । नमस्ते वायो । त्वामेव प्रत्यक्षम् ब्रह्म असि ।
namo brahmaṇe, namaste vāyo, tvām-eva pratyakṣam brahma- asi,
bow- to Brahman, bow- to prana, you-really- visible- Brahman- are
Prostrations to Absolute Reality! Prostrations to Vayu, the prana, who is really the visible Absolute Reality.

त्वामेव प्रत्यक्षम् ब्रह्म वदिष्यामि ऋतम् वदिष्यामि
tvām-eva pratyakṣam brahma vadiṣyāmi ṛtam vadiṣyāmi
you- really- visible Brahman- I declare-are- my inner Truth- I declare
Really, I proclaim prana is the visible Brahman. I declare my inner experience Truth.

सत्यम् वदिष्यामि । तन् माम् अवतु तद् वक्तारम् अवतु
satyam vadiṣyāmi, tan mām-avatu, tad-vaktāram avatu
Truth always to all- I declare. That- protect me- That- the teacher- protect
I declare it is Truth always for all. May you protect me. May you protect the teacher.

अवतु माम् । अवतु वक्तारम् ॥
avatu mām, avatu vaktāram.
protect- me- protect- the teacher
Protect me. Protect the teacher.

ॐ शान्तिः शान्तिः शान्तिः
om śāntiḥ śāntiḥ śāntiḥ
Om, peace, peace, peace.

O Self-Luminosity!

Strengthen my limbs, speech, life force,
eyes, ears, and let all my senses be strong.
Everything is Absolute Reality,
as proclaimed in the Upanisads.
May I never neglect Absolute Reality.
Do not, do not, O Absolute Reality,
ever neglect me.
May I never reject Absolute Reality.
May Absolute Reality never reject me.
I delight in the oneness of Paramatma and Atman.
Let all the virtues of the Upanisads
reside in me, reside in me.

Om, peace, peace, peace.

9. Plea for Strength and Virtue

ॐ
om
O Self-Luminosity!

आप्यायन्तु ममांगानि वाक् प्राणश् चक्षुः श्रोत्रम् अथो बलम् इन्द्रियाणि च सर्वाणि।
āpyāyantu mamāṅgāni vāk- prāṇaś- cakṣuḥ śrotram- atho balam- indriyāṇi ca sarvāṇi,
strengthen- my limbs- speech- life force- eyes- ears- also- strong- senses- and- all
Strengthen my limbs, speech, life force, eyes, ears, and let all my senses be strong.

सर्वम् ब्रह्म उपनिषदम्
sarvam brahma- upaniṣadam
all- Brahma- Upanisad-said in.
Everything is Absolute Reality, as proclaimed in the Upanisads.

मा अहम् ब्रह्म निराकुर्याम्
mā- aham brahma nirākuryām
I do not- Brahma- neglect
May I never neglect Absolute Reality.

मा मा ब्रह्म निराकरोद् अनिराकरणम् अस्तु अनिराकरणम् मे अस्तु
mā mā brahma nirākarod- anirākaraṇam- astu- anirākaraṇam me astu
do not- do not- Brahma- neglect no rejection- let it be, no rejection- to me-let it be
Do not, do not, Absolute Reality, ever neglect me. May I never reject Absolute Reality. May Absolute Reality never reject me.

तद् आत्मनि निरते य
tad-ātmani nirate ya
that- Atman- I delight in which-
I delight in the oneness of Paramatma and Atman.

उपनिषत्सु धर्मास् ते मयि सन्तु ते मयि सन्तु ॥
upaniṣatsu dharmās- te mayi santu te mayi santu
in the Upanisads- virtues let them be- in me- let them be- in me
Let all the virtues of the Upanisads reside in me, reside in me.

ॐ शान्तिः शान्तिः शान्तिः
om śāntiḥ śāntiḥ śāntiḥ
Om, peace, peace, peace.

O Self-Luminosity!

That is Perfect.
This is Perfect.
Perfect came out of perfect.
When perfect has been taken from perfect,
Perfect itself remains.

Om, peace, peace, peace.

10. Proclamation of Perfection

ॐ

om

O Self-Luminosity!

पूर्णम्   अदः   पूर्णम् इदम्

pūrṇam-   adaḥ   pūrṇam- idam

perfect-   that-   perfect- this

That is Perfect. This is Perfect.

पूर्णात्   पूण म्   उद ते ।

pūrṇat-   pūrṇam-   udacyate,

from perfect- perfect-   came out

Perfect came out of perfect.

पूर्णस्य   पूर्णम   आदाय

pūrṇasya   pūrṇam-   ādāya

from perfect- perfect-   having taken

When perfect has been taken from perfect,

पूर्णम्   एव   अवशिष्यते ॥

pūrṇam-   eva-   avaśiṣyate.

perfect-   itself- remains always.

Perfect itself remains.

ॐ शान्तिः शान्तिः शान्तिः

om śāntiḥ śāntiḥ śāntiḥ

Om, peace, peace, peace.

1. Call for Guidance to the Source

ॐ यो वै ब्रह्माणं विदधाति पूर्वं
यो वै वेदांश्च प्रहिणोति तस्मै ।

तं ह देवमात्मबुद्धिप्रकाशं
मुमुक्षुर्वै शरणमहं प्रपद्ये ॥

ॐ शान्तिः शान्तिः शान्तिः ॥

2. Request for Wisdom and Protection

ॐ वाङ्मे मनसि प्रतिष्ठिता मनो मे वाचि प्रतिष्ठितमाविराविर्म एधि ।

वेदस्य मा आणीस्थः श्रुतं मे मा प्रहासीरनेनाधीतेनाहोरात्रान्संदधाम्यृतं वदिष्यामि ।

सत्यं वदिष्यामि तन्मामवतु । तद्वक्तारमवतु । अवतु मामवतु वक्तारं अवतु वक्तारम् ॥

ॐ शान्तिः शान्तिः शान्तिः ॥

3. Petition for Auspiciousness

ॐ भद्रं कर्णेभिः श्रृणुयाम देवाः । भद्रं पश्येमाक्षभिर्यजत्राः ।

स्थिरैरंगैस्तुष्टुवांसस्तनूभिः । व्यशेम देवहितं यदायुः ॥

ॐ शान्तिः शान्तिः शान्तिः ॥

4. Student Teacher Agreement

ॐ सह नाववतु । सह नौ भुनक्तु । सह वीर्यं करवावहै ।

तेजस्वि नावधीतमस्तु मा विद्विषावहै ॥

ॐ शान्तिः शान्तिः शान्तिः ॥

5. Request for Knowledge of Reality

ॐ यश्छन्दसामृषभो विश्वरूपः ॥ छन्दोभ्योऽध्यमृतात्संबभूव । समेन्द्रो मेधया स्पृणोतु ॥

अमृतस्य देव धारणो भूयासम् ॥ शरीरं मे विचर्षणम् ॥ जिह्वा मे मधुमत्तमा ॥

कर्णाभ्यां भूरि विश्रुवम् ॥ ब्रह्मणः कोशोऽसि मेधया पिहितः ॥ श्रुतं मे गोपाय ॥

ॐ शान्तिः शान्तिः शान्तिः ॥

6. Asking for Peaceful Adjuncts

ॐ भद्रं नो अपिवातय मनः ॥

ॐ शान्तिः शान्तिः शान्तिः ॥

7. Trishanku's Declaration

ॐ अहं वृक्षस्य रेरिव । कीर्त्तिः कीर्त्तिह् पृष्ठं गिरेरिव ।

उर्ध्वपवित्रो वाजिनीव स्वमृतमस्मि । द्रविणं सवर्चसम् ।

सुमेधा अमृतोऽक्षितः । इति त्रिशंकोर्वेदानुवचनम् ॥

ॐ शान्तिः शान्तिः शान्तिः ॥

8. Praise and Prostrations

ॐ शं नो मित्रः शं वरुणः। शं नो भवत्वर्यमा ।

शं न इन्द्रो बृहस्पतिः । शं नो विष्णुरुरुक्रमः ।

नमो ब्रह्मणे । नमस्ते वायो । त्वमेव प्रत्यक्षं ब्रह्मासि ।

त्वामेव प्रत्यक्षं ब्रह्म वदिष्यामि ऋतं वदिष्यामि सत्यं वदिष्यामि ।

तन्मामवतु । तद्वक्तारमवतु अवतु मां । अवतु वक्तारम् ॥

ॐ शान्तिः शान्तिः शान्तिः ॥

9. Plea for Strength and Virtue

ॐ आप्यायन्तु ममांगानि वाक्प्राणश्चक्षुः श्रोत्रमथो बलमिन्द्रियाणि च सर्वाणि ।

सर्वं ब्रह्मौपनिषदं माहं ब्रह्म निराकुर्यं मा मा ब्रह्म निराकरोदनिराकरणमस्त्वनिराकरणं मे अस्तु ।

तदात्मनि निरते य उपनिषत्सु धर्मास्ते मयि सन्तु ते मयि सन्तु ॥

ॐ शान्तिः शान्तिः शान्तिः ॥

10. Proclamation of Perfection

ॐ पूर्णमदः पूर्णमिदं पूर्णात्पूर्णमुदच्यते ।

पूर्णस्य पूर्णमादाय पूर्णमेवावशिष्यते ॥

ॐ शान्तिः शान्तिः शान्तिः ॥

1. Call for Guidance to the Source

With my whole heart
strongly burning for liberation,
I really yearn for help and guidance
from that Luminosity, the One—
who truly ordained the Creator
in the beginning of creation,
who truly revealed to him
knowledge of the four Vedas,
and whose effulgence truly illumines
our individual intelligence—
that I may return to the Source,
that very Luminosity Itself.
Om, peace, peace, peace.

2. Request for Wisdom and Protection

Let my speech be rooted in my mind.
Let my mind be rooted in my speech.
Brahman! Brahman! Reveal Thyself to me!
Bless me with the knowledge of my ancestors.
Let my education never forget me.
I will reflect day and night on what I learned.
I will report my inner experience of liberation,
which this knowledge brought forth.
I will declare it is the Truth possible for all.
May you protect me.
May you protect my teacher.
Protect me. Protect my teacher.
Protect my teacher.
Om, peace, peace, peace.

3. Petition for Auspiciousness

O adorable devas, beings of light!
May my ears always hear what is auspicious.
May my eyes always see what is auspicious.
I glorify you with my strong body and mind.
May I live in the way of Illumination
for all of my allotted lifetime.
Om, peace, peace, peace.

4. Student Teacher Agreement

May we both be protected.
May we both grow and improve together.
May we both have strong motivation for our endeavor.
May our knowledge brightly shine, and
May we thus always have harmony
in our life together.
Om, peace, peace, peace.

5. Request for Knowledge of Reality

As the bull is in the cow herd,
so the monosyllable om is in the Vedic hymns.
You are all-pervasive, the manifest knowledge of Immortality.
Like Indra, may I be prosperous with the knowledge of Reality.
O deva, bright being of Light!
Let me be the repository of the knowledge of immortality.
Let my body be strong for the spiritual endeavor.
Let my tongue be full of delight.
Let me be ananda, the experience beyond mind and senses.
Let my ears hear abundantly.
O Luminosity, you are clothed with sattvic wisdom.
These manifest adjuncts veil you,
but the knowledge of Reality adorns you.
Let me preserve what I have learned and
apply it to attain the goal.
Om, peace, peace, peace.

6. Asking for Peaceful Adjuncts

May our body,
senses, prana, mind,
and Intellect
be good to us.
Om, peace, peace, peace.

7. Trishanku's Declaration

I am the feller of the trees of samskara!
I am the prestige of the mountaintop of realization!
I am great purity like the sun!
I am the knowledge of Reality!
I am the greatest treasure of all!
I am all wise, immortal, imperishable!
This is the revelation Trishanku
proclaimed in the Veda.
Om, peace, peace, peace.

8. Praise and Prostrations

Morning sun, be good to us.
Midday sun, be good to us.
Evening sun, be good to us.
Indra, king of the devas, be good to us.
Brihaspati, Lord of knowledge, be good to us.
Vishnu, the all-pervasive, grant us speedy progress.
Prostrations to Absolute Reality!
Prostrations to Vayu, the prana,
who is really the visible Absolute Reality.
Really, I proclaim prana is the visible Brahman.
I declare my inner experience is Truth.
I declare it is Truth always for all.
May you protect me.
May you protect the teacher.
Protect me. Protect the teacher.
Om, peace, peace, peace.

9. Plea for Strength and Virtue

Strengthen my limbs, speech, life force,
eyes, ears, and let all my senses be strong.
Everything is Absolute Reality,
as proclaimed in the Upanisads.
May I never neglect Absolute Reality.
Do not, do not, O Absolute Reality,
ever neglect me.
May I never reject Absolute Reality.
May Absolute Reality never reject me.
I delight in the oneness of Paramatma and
Atman.
Let all the virtures of the Upanisads
reside in me, reside in me.
Om, peace, peace, peace.

10. Proclamation of Perfection

That is Perfect.
This is Perfect.
Perfect came out of perfect.
When perfect has been taken from perfect,
Perfect itself remains.
Om, peace, peace, peace.

1. Call for Guidance to the Source

om yo vai brahmāṇam vidadhāti pūrvam
yo vai vedāmś-ca prahinoti tasmai,
tam ha devam-ātma-buddhi-prakāśam
mumukṣur-vai śaraṇam-aham prapadye.
om śāntiḥ śāntiḥ śāntiḥ

2. Request for Wisdom and Protection

om vāṅ-me manasi pratiṣṭhitā
mano me vāci pratiṣṭhitam āvir-āvir ma edhi,
vedasya ma āṇīsthaḥ śrutam me mā prahāsīr-
anena-adhītena-ahorātrān-sandadhāmi
ṛtam vadiṣyāmi, satyam vadiṣyāmi
tan-mām-avatu tad-vaktāram-avatu,
avatu mām-avatu vaktāram avatu vaktāram.
om śāntiḥ śāntiḥ śāntiḥ

3. Petition for Auspiciousness

om bhadram karṇebhiḥ śṛṇuyāma devāḥ,
bhadram paśyema-akṣabhir-yajatrāḥ,
stiraiраṅgais-tuṣṭuvāṅ-gaṁ-sastanūbhiḥ,
vyaśema deva-hitam yad-āyuḥ.
om śāntiḥ śāntiḥ śāntiḥ

4. Student Teacher Agreement

om saha na-avavatu,
saha nau bhunāktu,
saha vīryam karavāvahai,
tejasvi na-avadhītam-astu
mā vidviṣāvahai.
om śāntiḥ śāntiḥ śāntiḥ

5. Request for Knowledge of Reality

om yaś-chandasām-ṛsabho visvarūpaḥ.
chandobhyo adhyamṛtāt-sambabhūva,
samendro medhayā spṛṇotu.
amṛtasya deva dhāraṇo bhūyāsam.
śarīram me vicarṣaṇam.
jihvā me madhumattamā.
karṇābhyām bhūri viśruvam.
brahmaṇaḥ kośo'si medhayā pihitaḥ.
śrutam me gopāya.
om śāntiḥ śāntiḥ śāntiḥ

6. Asking for Peaceful Adjuncts

om bhadram no apivātaya manaḥ.
om śāntiḥ śāntiḥ śāntiḥ

7. Trishanku's Declaration

om aham vṛkśasya reriva,
kīrttiḥ pṛṣṭham gireriva,
ūrdhva-pavitro vājinīva svam-ṛtam-asmi,
draviṇam savarcasam,
sumedhā amṛto'kṣitaḥ,
iti triśaṅkor-veda-anuvācanam.
om śāntiḥ śāntiḥ śāntiḥ

8. Praise and Prostrations

om śam no mitraḥ śam varuṇaḥ,
śam no bhavatvaryamā,
śam na indro bṛhaspatiḥ,
śam no viṣṇur-urukramaḥ,
namo brahmaṇe, namaste vāyo,
tvam-eva pratyakṣam brahmāsi,
tvam-eva pratyakṣam brahma vadiṣyāmi
ṛtam vadiṣyāmi satyam vadiṣyāmi,
tanmām-avatu, tad-vaktāram-avatu
avatu mām, avatu vaktāram.
om śāntiḥ śāntiḥ śāntiḥ

9. Plea for Strength and Virtue

om āpyāyantu mamāṅgāni vākprāṇaścakṣuḥ
śrotramatho balamindriyāṇi ca sarvāṇi,
sarvam brahmaupaniṣadam
mā-aham brahma nirākuryām
mā mā brahma nirākarod-
anirākaraṇam-astu-anirākaraṇam me astu,
tadātmani nirate ya upaniṣatsu dharmās
te mayi santu te mayi santu.
om śāntiḥ śāntiḥ śāntiḥ

10. Proclamation of Perfection

om pūrṇam adaḥ pūrṇam idam
pūrṇāt-pūrṇam-udacyate,
pūrṇasya pūrṇamādāya
pūrṇam-eva-avaśiṣyate.
om śāntiḥ śāntiḥ śāntiḥ

The verses of and commentary on ten Upanisads affiliated with the shanti mantras presented in this booklet can be found in Swami Sivananda's *Ten Upanisads*, published by The Divine Life Society.

Patanjali Kundalini Yoga–Care is a spiritual guidance service for qualified spiritual seekers. Based on Traditional Kundalini Science (Kundalini Vidya), it supports serious aspirants in advancing their spiritual progress by providing individualized spiritual practices designed for their particular needs. The specialty of PKYC is to assess the kind of spiritual process that seekers have, to assist them in reaching a stable higher level, and to support them in their continued spiritual advancement by providing ongoing spiritual education, consultations, recommendations, and guidance so they can progress more skillfully and dedicatedly. This helps the divine within make efficient, untroubled, and speedy progress toward Liberation, awareness of oneness with the One.

FOR MORE INFORMATION VISIT: KundaliniCare.com

Made in the USA
Las Vegas, NV
10 January 2022

41041325R00020